Monster Dinosaurs

KINGFISHER

First published 2016 by Kingfisher
an imprint of Macmillan Children's Books
20 New Wharf Road, London N1 9RR
Associated companies throughout the world
www.panmacmillan.com

Interior design by Tall Tree Ltd
Cover design by Peter Clayman

Adapted from an original text by David Burnie
Literacy consultants: Kerenza Ghosh, Stephanie Laird

Illustrations by Sam and Steve Weston
Gary Hanna/www.the-art-agency.co.uk
Peter Bull Art Studio

ISBN 978-0-7534-3963-0

A CIP catalogue record for this book is available from the British Library.

Printed in China

9 8 7 6 5 4 3 2 1
1TR/1115/WKT/UG/128MA

Picture credits
The Publisher would like to thank the following for permission to reproduce their material.
Top = t; Bottom = b; Centre = c; Left = l; Right = r
All cover images Kingfisher Artbank; Page 29 Getty/National Geographic Society; 7t Corbis/Louie
Psihoyos; 9c Corbis/Louie Psihoyos/Science Faction; 9b Natural History Museum, London;
14 Corbis/Louie Psihoyos; 21 Corbis/Louie Psihoyos; 23 Getty/Dorling Kindersley; 24 Corbis/Louie
Psihoyos; 27 Corbis/Michael and Patricia Fogden.

Contents

Age of the dinosaurs

period
In geological time, a period is a smaller part of an era. A period may last up to 100 million years.

The Dinosaur Age lasted over 160 million years. During that time, dinosaurs **evolved** many different shapes and ways of living. Some moved on all fours and ate plants, while others ran on their back legs and hunted other animals.

tyrannosaurs
('ti-ran-oh-saws')

allosaurs
('al-loh-saws')

ceratosaurs
('seh-ra-toh-saws')

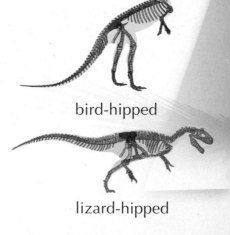

The big split
Early on in their history, dinosaurs split into two different types. Lizard-hipped dinosaurs included all the meat-eaters, as well as the enormous plant-eaters called sauropods. All bird-hipped dinosaurs were plant-eaters.

bird-hipped

lizard-hipped

birds

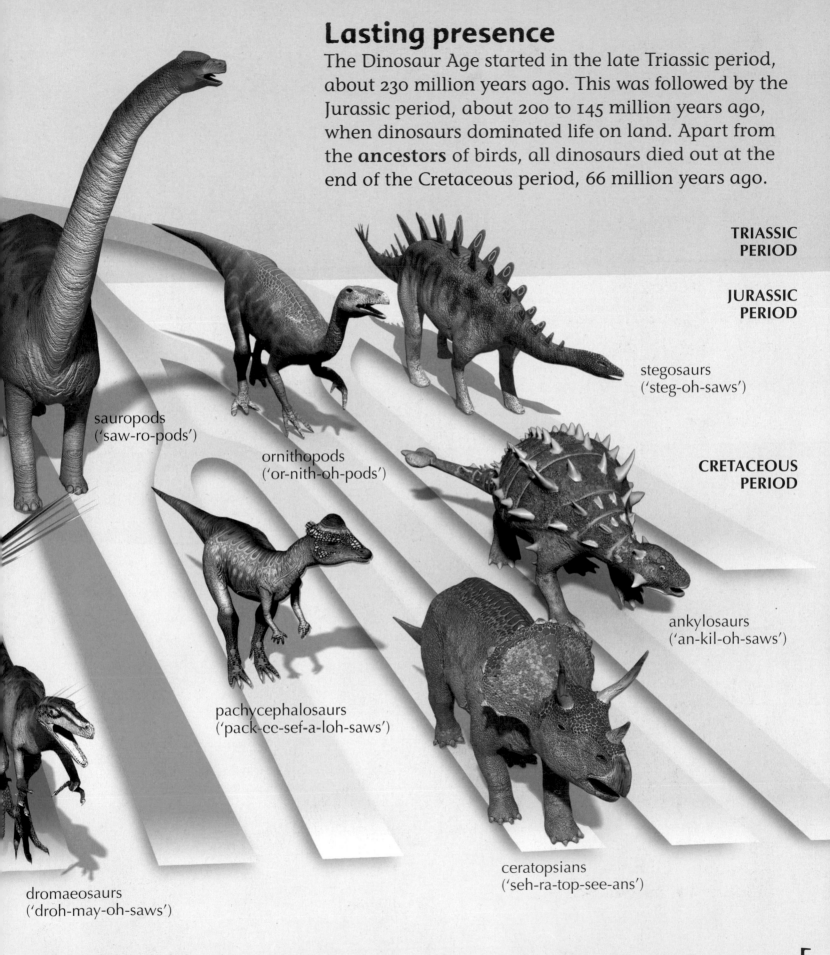

Lasting presence

The Dinosaur Age started in the late Triassic period, about 230 million years ago. This was followed by the Jurassic period, about 200 to 145 million years ago, when dinosaurs dominated life on land. Apart from the **ancestors** of birds, all dinosaurs died out at the end of the Cretaceous period, 66 million years ago.

TRIASSIC PERIOD

JURASSIC PERIOD

CRETACEOUS PERIOD

stegosaurs
('steg-oh-saws')

sauropods
('saw-ro-pods')

ornithopods
('or-nith-oh-pods')

ankylosaurs
('an-kil-oh-saws')

pachycephalosaurs
('pack-cc-sef-a-loh-saws')

ceratopsians
('seh-ra-top-see-ans')

dromaeosaurs
('droh-may-oh-saws')

Early dinosaurs

The world's first dinosaurs appeared about 230 million years ago. At first, they were quite small. One of the oldest dinosaurs found so far is a creature called *Eoraptor* ('ee-oh-rap-tor'). It was a fast-moving, lightweight **theropod**, and was about one metre long.

flexible
Able to bend or move easily, in order to grasp or catch with fingers, for example.

slim, mobile neck

Flexible hands have fingers for grasping.

This *Eoraptor* is carrying off a lizard it has just caught.

TOP FIVE BITESIZE FACTS

- The name *Eoraptor* means 'dawn raider'.

- Fossils of *Eoraptor* have been found in a place called Valley of the Moon in northwestern Argentina.

- Each of *Eoraptor*'s hands had five fingers.

- Three of these fingers had long claws. The other two were too small to be of any use.

- An *Eoraptor* weighed about 10 kilograms, which is the weight of a small dog.

Treasure trove

Eoraptor lived alongside another early dinosaur called *Herrerasaurus* ('heh-reh-ra-sau-rus'). Both dinosaurs lived about 228 million years ago. *Herrerasaurus* was much bigger than *Eoraptor*, and measured up to six metres long.

Herrerasaurus skull

Tail used as balance for head and neck.

Ankles let feet bend up or down.

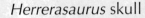

Three toes to make contact with the ground.

Fast hunter

Eoraptor sprinted on strong back legs. It stood upright and had small arms. This dinosaur died out about 225 million years ago, but theropods went on to include giants such as *Tyrannosaurus rex* – one of the biggest **predators** that has ever walked the Earth.

Chisel-shaped teeth with wide tips pulled off leaves, but did not chew.

sauropod
A plant-eating dinosaur with a huge body and a very long neck and tail.

Brachiosaurus ('bra-kee-oh-saw-rus')

Giant plant-eaters

Plant-eating dinosaurs called sauropods were the largest animals ever to have walked the Earth. The longest measured up to 40 metres from head to tail – the length of four buses. They may have weighed over 100 tonnes.

These leaves were hard, and often ended in sharp points.

TOP FIVE BITESIZE FACTS

- Fully grown brachiosaurs could reach twice as high as a giraffe.
- Brachiosaurs used their teeth like a rake to tear off mouthfuls of leaves.
- The stones swallowed by dinosaurs to help them grind up food are called **gastroliths**.
- Fossilized dinosaur droppings are known as **coprolites**.
- Coprolites can be over 60 centimetres long.

Stomach stones

Instead of chewing, many dinosaurs swallowed stones to help them grind up food inside their stomach.

Head for heights

In this scene from the late Jurassic period, about 160 million years ago, a herd of brachiosaurs are feeding on leaves from trees. Brachiosaurs had extra-large front legs, which helped to make them 12 metres tall – seven times the height of an adult human.

Dinosaur droppings

Large dinosaurs had to eat an enormous amount of food to keep themselves alive. Scientists know what dinosaurs ate by looking at the fossilized remains of their droppings.

These fossilized dinosaur droppings were probably made by a sauropod called *Titanosaurus* ('ty-tan-oh-saw-rus').

Dinosaur tracks

When scientists first studied dinosaur tracks, they thought they belonged to huge flightless birds. Since then, these fascinating 'trace **fossils**' have been identified and found all over the world.

trace fossil
Preserved remains of things left behind by animals.

Traces in time
Walking across the bed of a desert lake, these three dinosaurs left very different tracks in the mud. The *Apatosaurus* ('a-pat-oh-saw-rus') left rounded tracks, while *Gallimimus* ('ga-lee-my-mus') and *Dryosaurus* ('dry-oh-saw-rus') left three-toed prints. The faster they ran, the deeper their toes dug into the mud.

Apatosaurus took strides that were up to five metres long.

Gallimimus could run at speeds of over 50 kilometres per hour in short bursts.

Gallimimus and other theropods left three-toed prints.

Sauropod prints are deep and round. The rear feet left claw marks, but the front ones often did not.

Dryosaurus had short arms, and ran on its back legs.

When *Dryosaurus* ran quickly, its footprints were spaced far apart.

Footprint to fossil

To fossilize, tracks first have to harden by drying in the sun. Next they are filled in by layers of mud. As the mud builds up, it is slowly squeezed into rock. After millions of years, the rock wears away, leaving behind a fossil footprint.

1. Footprint is left in the mud.

2. Footprint fills up with more mud.

3. Over millions of years, the mud turns to rock.

4. Material filling the footprint washes out, leaving a fossilized track.

Eggs and babies

Dinosaurs bred by laying eggs, like most reptiles do today. At Egg Mountain, in the US state of Montana, a herd of duck-billed dinosaurs nested together. Fossils show that the parent dinosaurs took care of their eggs. They also collected food for the newly hatched young.

Family group

A mother *Maiasaura* ('my-yah-saw-rah') looks after her eggs and young. These dinosaurs made bowl-shaped nests and lined them with plants, which helped to keep the eggs warm. Fossils show that the young were very small when they hatched. Their parents would have to bring the babies food for them to survive.

Females nested at the same time, making it harder for predators to reach the eggs or young.

Long drop

Small and medium-sized dinosaurs could squat to lay their eggs. However, giant sauropods, such as *Apatosaurus*, could hardly bend their back legs. Their eggs faced a drop of two metres or more before they hit the ground – that's taller than an adult human! To stop them breaking, female sauropods may have had a fleshy egg-laying tube, called an ovipositor ('oh-vee-posit-or').

Nest was made from earth scraped into a ring.

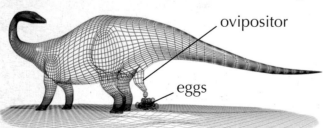

ovipositor

eggs

Apatosaurus

Nests were neatly spaced in the colony.

TOP FIVE BITESIZE FACTS

- Dinosaur eggs ranged in size from the width of a tennis ball to 40 centimetres across — the same size as a beach ball.

- Some dinosaurs laid more than 20 eggs at a time.

- The name *Maiasaura* means 'good mother'.

- The first discovery of dinosaur egg fossils was made in 1859 — they were thought to have been laid by giant birds.

- Some dinosaurs laid their eggs in neat circles, while others laid them in untidy piles.

Young probably stayed in the nest for several weeks.

incubate
To keep eggs warm after they have been laid, allowing them to develop and hatch.

Plants created heat as they rotted, incubating the eggs.

13

Dino attack

Some meat-eating dinosaurs worked like wolves in a pack to hunt **prey** much bigger than themselves. One of these was *Deinonychus* ('die-noh-ny-cus'). It used large claws to attack its victims. *Deinonychus* was light enough to leap on the back of its prey.

About 100 million years ago, this plant-eating *Tenontosaurus* ('ten-on-toh-saw-rus') fell prey to an attacking pack of *Deinonychus*.

swivel
When one part rotates while the other part stays still, such as the slashing motion of the claw on the foot of *Deinonychus*.

Deinonychus

Hands had three fingers with long claws.

Feathered predator

Deinonychus belonged to the dromaeosaurids ('droh-mayo-saw-rids'), a family of fast, light predators. Scientists have found some of these creatures with fossilized feathers. *Deinonychus* probably had feathers and was **warm-blooded**. With its birdlike body, *Deinonychus* may have been an ancestor of today's birds.

TOP FIVE **BITESIZE** FACTS

🦴 *Deinonychus* was about 3 metres long.

🦴 Warm-blooded dinosaurs, such as *Deinonychus*, could stay active even in cold conditions.

🦴 Warm-blooded dinosaurs also needed to consume more food for energy, so *Deinonychus* packs were always on the hunt for prey.

🦴 The name *Deinonychus* means 'terrible claw'.

🦴 The extra-long claw on *Deinonychus* measured 12 centimetres.

Second toe swivelled downwards when *Deinonychus* attacked, providing a hooked grip.

Tenontosaurus

Large claw on second toe stayed off the ground when *Deinonychus* was on the move, keeping it sharp.

Huge rear leg muscles supported *Tyrannosaurus rex* while it fed.

Skin may have had feathers.

Feeding time

Tyrannosaurus rex bit and tore at its food. It could rip off up to 75 kilograms of flesh in a single bite – that's about the same weight as an adult human. It had a very keen sense of smell, which helped it to track down its food.

Skull had large holes between bones to reduce weight of head.

Teeth at front of jaw curved backwards.

scavenger
An animal that feeds on the remains of dead creatures.

Hunter on two legs

Tyrannosaurus rex is the world's most famous predator. We know what it looked like thanks to some incredible fossil finds. One of them, nicknamed 'Sue', is very well preserved – a sign that it was covered by mud or sand very soon after it died. The lifestyle of *Tyrannosaurus rex* remains a puzzle. Some scientists believe it hunted for its food, while others think it may have been a scavenger.

TOP FIVE BITESIZE FACTS

> *Tyrannosaurus rex* had teeth that were up to 30 centimetres long.

> It was about 12 metres long and stood up to 6 metres tall – taller than a giraffe.

> Its arms were too short to reach its mouth but could be used to grab prey.

> Its bite was so powerful that it could break and crush the bones of anything it ate.

> *Tyrannosaurus rex* became extinct at the end of the Cretaceous period, 66 million years ago.

17

Under attack

Plant-eating dinosaurs had many ways of defending themselves against meat-eaters. Some hit back by rearing up on their back legs, or by stabbing with sharp claws. *Ankylosaurus* ('an-kill-oh-saw-rus') was covered in armour, and had a huge club at the end of its tail.

Scissor claws

Therizinosaurus ('the-ri-zin-oh-saw-rus') had enormous claws. They could be used as weapons to attack or defend.

Ankylosaurus

Killer blow

Ankylosaurus was built to stand and fight rather than to run away. Here, the dinosaur is fighting off an *Albertosaurus* ('al-ber-toh-saw-rus'). *Ankylosaurus*'s skin was protected with bony plates, and its tail club could swing if anything came too close. Its only weak point was its underside, which had unarmoured skin.

Albertosaurus

Rows of large
plates ran along
back and sides.

Skin protected
by bony plates
and knobs called
osteoderms.

Tail club
weighed over
50 kilograms.

armour
Tough, hard skin or spikes
used for defence against
predator attacks.

Bony plates
protected
each eye.

TOP FIVE BITESIZE FACTS

Ankylosaurus weighed about 5 tonnes — that's
more than twice the weight of a rhinoceros.

The name *Ankylosaurus* means 'fused lizard'.

It lived during the late Cretaceous period in what
is now the western USA and Canada.

Ankylosaurus measured up to 10 metres from the
tip of its head to the end of its tail.

Ankylosaurus had some of the smallest teeth in
the dinosaur world in comparison to its size.

19

TOP FIVE BITESIZE FACTS

- *Triceratops* could weigh as much as 6 tonnes — the same as a large elephant.

- Its name means 'three-horned face'.

- Its skull could measure 2.5 metres long — that's taller than an adult human. It was the largest ever skull grown by a land animal.

- *Styracosaurus* was smaller than *Triceratops*, but it still weighed nearly 3 tonnes.

- The neck frill of *Styracosaurus* had at least four enormous spikes.

Locking horns

These two male *Triceratops* are struggling to be the top dinosaur in their herd. In contests such as these, males would probably have rammed their opponents. These battles could cause nasty injuries, and some fossil skulls show deep scratches and gouges where the horns hit.

Horns and shields

Triceratops ('try-seh-ra-tops') had three horns and a huge head shield. This plant-eater lived towards the end of the Dinosaur Age and belonged to a family of dinosaurs known as **ceratopsians**. It used its horns to defend itself and to battle with other *Triceratops*.

frill
The large shield found on the back of the head of some dinosaurs.

Two male *Triceratops* clash in a fight of dominance.

Head gear

The head shield of a ceratopsian could be twice the size of a car door. The frill of a *Triceratops* was made of solid bone, which meant that it was extremely heavy. *Styracosaurus* ('sti-rah-coh-saw-rus') had two gaps in its frill, which made it lighter.

Fish-eating dinosaurs

Baryonyx ('ba-ree-oh-nix') lived on land but hunted for fish in rivers and lakes. As soon as a fish was close enough, it would strike with its jaws or hook the fish with its long front claws.

Sudden death

Baryonyx had crocodile-like jaws. It caught small fish using only its teeth, but used its claws to catch bigger fish. The claws stabbed the fish and then swept it out of the water and onto dry land.

Teeth had very long roots buried deep into the skull.

Lucky find

Baryonyx was found by an amateur fossil hunter in 1983. He spotted one of its claws in a clay pit in southern England – the site had been a river estuary when *Baryonyx* was alive. Nearby was most of its skeleton, which had been buried for more than 125 million years.

estuary
The mouth of a river where it meets the sea.

Catfish were slow moving, making them easy to catch.

23

Early bird

The world's oldest fossil of a true bird was found in Germany, in 1861. It was called *Archaeopteryx* ('ar-kee-op-ter-ix') and it had teeth, clawed wings and a long tail. It looked like a small theropod dinosaur, but it had feathers and could fly.

TOP FIVE BITESIZE FACTS

- *Caudipteryx* first appeared in the early Cretaceous period, about 125 million years ago.

- The first fossils of *Caudipteryx* were found in the late 1990s.

- *Archaeopteryx* lived about 150 million years ago.

- It was about 50 centimetres long and weighed less than 1 kilogram.

- The name *Archaeopteryx* comes from ancient Greek words meaning 'ancient wing'.

Outstretched arms also helped to sweep insects towards the jaws.

Dinobirds

In recent years, scientists have found fossils of dinosaurs with feathers. The earliest kinds had short and simple feathers, which worked like a coat of fur. Over time, these became more like the flight feathers that birds have today.

Bird-like beak had a small number of simple teeth.

flight feather
A feather with a special shape that creates **lift**, a force that helps a bird to fly.

High-speed chase
Swerving after a dragonfly, this *Caudipteryx* ('cor-dip-ter-ix') stretches out its feathered arms as it reaches for its prey. *Caudipteryx* could not fly, but its feathered arms and tail helped it to steer. Its body was covered with short feathers, **insulating** it to keep it warm.

Disaster!

Throughout the Dinosaur Age, new kinds of dinosaurs slowly appeared and old ones became **extinct**. But 66 million years ago, all the dinosaurs vanished. This disaster was probably caused by a huge collision between the Earth and a **meteorite** from space.

As well as dinosaurs, the impact killed flying reptiles, or **pterosaurs** ('te-roh-saws'), and many of the reptiles that lived in the seas.

Survivors

Some creatures did survive the impact, such as birds, **mammals** and some **reptiles**. The surviving reptiles included crocodiles, tortoises, tuataras and the ancestors of today's snakes and lizards.

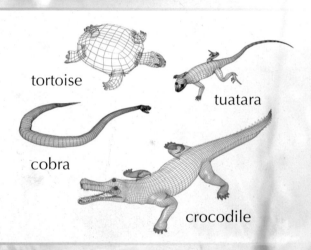

tortoise

tuatara

cobra

crocodile

Triceratops

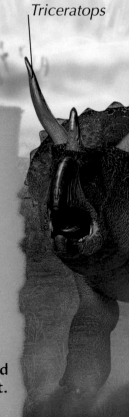

TOP FIVE BITESIZE FACTS

- Scientists believe that the meteorite impact happened off what is now the coast of Mexico.

- The remains of the **crater** left by the impact measure 180 kilometres across.

- The impact led to the extinction of about three-quarters of all types, or **species**, of plants and animals.

- Other survivors included snails and sea urchins.

- Some scientists believe the extinction was caused by volcanic eruptions rather than a single impact.

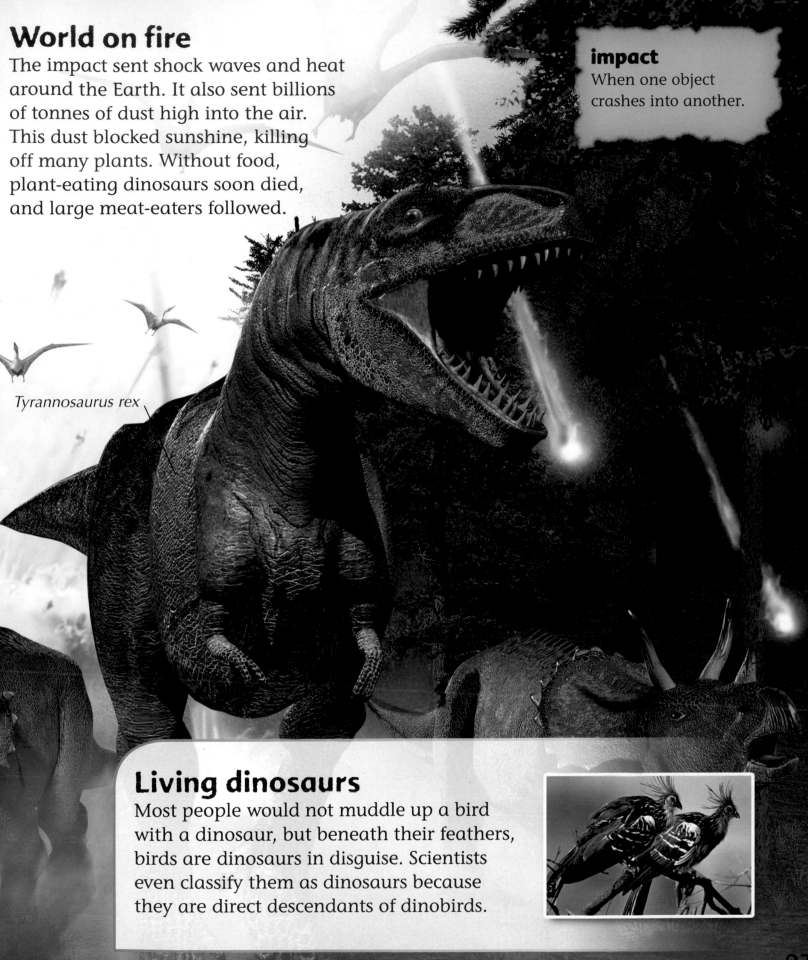

World on fire

The impact sent shock waves and heat around the Earth. It also sent billions of tonnes of dust high into the air. This dust blocked sunshine, killing off many plants. Without food, plant-eating dinosaurs soon died, and large meat-eaters followed.

Tyrannosaurus rex

impact
When one object crashes into another.

Living dinosaurs

Most people would not muddle up a bird with a dinosaur, but beneath their feathers, birds are dinosaurs in disguise. Scientists even classify them as dinosaurs because they are direct descendants of dinobirds.

27

Dinosaur remains

Almost everything known about dinosaurs comes from fossilized bones. Sometimes, these are found by accident, by amateur fossil hunters, but many are discovered by scientific experts, or **palaeontologists** ('pa-lay-on-toll-oh-gists'). In some places, hundreds of fossils are found together in huge 'dinosaur graveyards'.

Giant on show

The world's tallest dinosaur fossil is a *Giraffatitan* ('ji-raff-ah-ty-tan') in a museum in Berlin, Germany. It was found in Tanzania in East Africa, in the early 1900s. It is 12 metres tall – the same as a four-storey building.

How fossils form

Animals turn into fossils when their remains are covered by mud or sand. The soft body parts disintegrate, but the bones slowly turn to stone. More mud builds up on top of the bones. Over millions of years, the rock above **erodes** and the fossil is exposed.

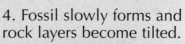

1. Dinosaur trapped by flood.

2. Body covered by water.

3. Mud covers remains.

4. Fossil slowly forms and rock layers become tilted.

5. Erosion exposes fossil.

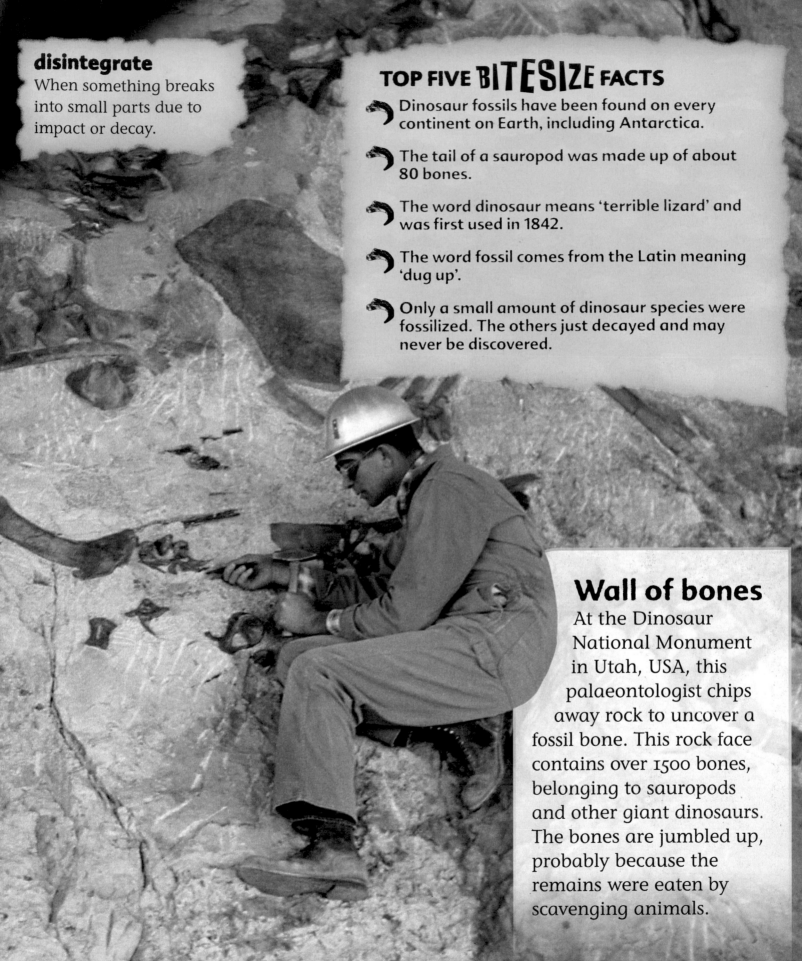

disintegrate
When something breaks into small parts due to impact or decay.

TOP FIVE BITESIZE FACTS

- Dinosaur fossils have been found on every continent on Earth, including Antarctica.

- The tail of a sauropod was made up of about 80 bones.

- The word dinosaur means 'terrible lizard' and was first used in 1842.

- The word fossil comes from the Latin meaning 'dug up'.

- Only a small amount of dinosaur species were fossilized. The others just decayed and may never be discovered.

Wall of bones

At the Dinosaur National Monument in Utah, USA, this palaeontologist chips away rock to uncover a fossil bone. This rock face contains over 1500 bones, belonging to sauropods and other giant dinosaurs. The bones are jumbled up, probably because the remains were eaten by scavenging animals.

29

Glossary

ancestor
An early kind of animal or plant. Dinosaurs are the ancestors of modern birds.

ceratopsian
A plant-eating dinosaur with a body like a rhinoceros. It had horns, and a bony head shield or frill.

coprolites
The fossilized remains of animal droppings.

crater
A circular hollow, created by a volcanic eruption or by a meteorite hitting the Earth.

erode
To gradually wear away. Rocks are eroded mainly by wind and rain, and also by frost splitting them apart.

evolved
Slowly changed so that living things become better at survival. Animals and plants evolved over many generations, instead of during a single lifetime.

extinct
No longer living anywhere on Earth. Extinction can happen gradually, or in bursts that wipe out many forms of life.

fossil
Remains of living things that have been preserved in the ground. In most fossils, the original remains are replaced by hard minerals.

gastroliths
Stones swallowed by animals to help grind up their food.

insulating
Slowing down heat loss, so that something stays warm.

lift
A natural force that works against the pull of gravity and keeps a flying animal in the air.

mammal
An animal that has fur, and that feeds its young on milk. Unlike reptiles, almost all mammals give birth to live young.

meteorite
A rock from space that travels through the atmosphere and hits the Earth's surface.

palaeontologist

A scientist who studies prehistoric life, using fossils and other kinds of evidence, such as footprints.

predator

An animal that attacks and kills other animals, and eats them for food.

prey

Animals that are hunted by other animals as food.

pterosaur

A reptile that flew on wings made of skin. Pterosaurs were not dinosaurs, but they lived alongside them.

reptile

An animal with scaly skin that lays eggs or gives birth to live young. Reptiles include snakes, lizards, tortoises and crocodiles, as well as dinosaurs.

species

A group of living things that look like each other, and that breed only with their own kind.

theropod

A dinosaur with small arms and hollow bones, which walked upright on its back legs. Most theropods were predators.

warm-blooded

An animal that keeps a constant body temperature even when the temperature outside is cold or hot.

Index